EXTREME NATURE

RAIN FOREST EXTREMES

JEN GREEN

Crabtree Publishing Company

www.crabtreebooks.com

Crabtree Publishing Company

www.crabtreebooks.com

Author: Jen Green

Editor: Molly Aloian

Proofreaders: Adrianna Morganelli, Katherine Berti

Project coordinator: Robert Walker

Production coordinator: Margaret Amy Salter

Prepress technician: Margaret Amy Salter

Project editor: Tom Jackson

Designer: Lynne Lennon

Picture researchers: Sophie Mortimer, Sean Hannaway

Managing editor: Tim Harris

Art director: Jeni Child

Design manager: David Poole

Editorial director: Lindsey Lowe

Children's publisher: Anne O'Daly

Photographs:

Corbis: Hubert Stadler: page 27 (bottom)

FLPA: Fritz Polking: page 4 (bottom); Michael & Patricia Fogden: pages 4–5, 21 (bottom); Pete Oxford: page 5 (bottom); Konrad Wothe: page 9 (bottom); Frans Lanting: page 10 (bottom); Albert Visage: page 13 (bottom); Jurgen & Christine Sohns: page 15 (bottom); Siegfried Grassegger: page 20; Mark Moffett: page 22

NaturePL: John Water: page 9 (top); Tim MacMillan/John Downer Pr: page 14; Lynn M. Stone: page 17 (bottom); Nick Gordon: pages 18–19

Science Photo Library: Dr. Jeremy Burgess: page 7 (right); Claude Nuridsany & Marie Perennou: page 12 (top center); John Mitchell: page 21 (top); Norman Lightfoot: page 23 (bottom)

Shutterstock: Christophe Testi: page 6 (bottom); Ingus Rukis: pages 6–7; Jerome Scholler: pages 8–9, 27 (top); Aleksandar Milosevic: page 10 (top); Zeber: pages 10–11; Paul Chia: page 11 (bottom right); Dr. Morley Read: pages 12–13; Alvaro Pantoja: page 15 (top); Steffen Foerster Photography: page 17 (top); Mike Von Bergen: page 19 (top); Rsfatt: page 23 (top); Charles Taylor: page 24 (bottom left); Salamanderman: pages 24–25; ChipPix: page 25 (top); A. S. Zain: page 26; Martinique: page 28; Eric Gevaert: page 29 (top); Mark Aplet: page 29 (bottom)

Topfoto: Dinodia: page 16; The Image Works: page 19 (bottom)

Every effort has been made to trace the owners of copyrighted material.

Library and Archives Canada Cataloguing in Publication

Green, Jen
    Rain forest extremes / Jen Green.

(Extreme nature)
Includes index.
ISBN 978-0-7787-4504-4 (bound).--ISBN 978-0-7787-4521-1 (pbk.)

    1. Rain forest ecology--Juvenile literature. 2. Rain forest animals--Juvenile literature. 3. Rain forest plants--Juvenile literature. 4. Rain forests--Juvenile literature. I. Title. II. Series: Extreme nature (St. Catharines, Ont.)

QH541.5.R27G73 2008   j577.34   C2008-907339-8

Library of Congress Cataloging-in-Publication Data

Green, Jen.
  Rain forest extremes / Jen Green.
    p. cm. -- (Extreme nature)
  Includes index.
  ISBN 978-0-7787-4521-1 (pbk. : alk. paper) -- ISBN 978-0-7787-4504-4 (reinforced library binding : alk. paper)
  1. Rain forests. 2. Rain forest ecology. I. Title. II. Series.

  QH86.G715 2009
  578.734--dc22

        2008048642

Crabtree Publishing Company

www.crabtreebooks.com   1-800-387-7650

Published in Canada
Crabtree Publishing
616 Welland Ave.
St. Catharines, Ontario
L2M 5V6

Published in the United States
Crabtree Publishing
PMB16A
350 Fifth Ave., Suite 3308
New York, NY 10118

CONTENTS

INTRODUCTION

IMAGINE you are on a path with thick vegetation on both sides. Enormous trees soar upward all around you. Mossy logs are alive with insects and spiders. Clouds of flies buzz around your head, and the forest is full of strange sounds. This extreme environment is a rain forest.

GREEN BELT

Tropical rain forests grow in hot places that get a lot of rain. They form a green belt around Earth on either side of the **equator**. The largest rain forest is the Amazon of South America. There are also huge forests in Central America, West Africa, and Southeast Asia. Small areas of jungle grow in places such as India and northern Australia.

Vital Statistics

★ The largest rain forest in the world is the Amazon rain forest in South America. It would cover about two-thirds of the United States.

★ The Amazon River is 4,000 miles (6,437 km) long.

Mini rain forests grow on **tropical** islands and even in the spray of huge waterfalls, such as Victoria Falls in Africa.

◀ *Rain forest trees provide a lot of shade, but the jungle is not a cool place. It is so hot and steamy that your body gets very sweaty.*

FAST FACTS

★ Some rain forests grow in cold, wet places, such as the Pacific coast of Canada.

★ Jungles that grow on mountains are called cloud forests.

★ Mangrove forests (*below*) grow out of mud along the coast.

WATER EVERYWHERE

Rain forests receive a huge amount of rain. They get at least 78 inches (198 cm) of rain a year—that is nearly double the rainfall of Quebec City, Quebec, and ten times the amount that falls on Los Angeles, California.

HOT AIR

The air is always steamy in a rain forest, like a bathroom after a hot bath. With all that water, it is hardly surprising that countless streams and rivers flow through the rain forests. The Amazon River alone contains one-fifth of all the world's river water.

▼ The world's largest rivers—the Amazon and Congo—flow through rain forests.

WHY ARE RAIN FORESTS WET?

The rain that falls on rain forests comes from clouds that **evaporate** from oceans in the hot, tropical sunlight. Rain forests lie in the path of damp winds that blow in from the oceans. **Moisture** is also recycled within the forest. Plant roots soak up rain, and their leaves release it as **water vapor**. This vapor rises above the trees to form clouds that release even more rain.

LAB WORK

Potted plants recycle moisture just like trees in a rain forest. See this for yourself: water a potted plant and then place a plastic bag over it. Leave it in a warm place for a few hours. Moisture released from tiny holes in the leaves (right) gathers on the inside of the bag and runs back into the soil.

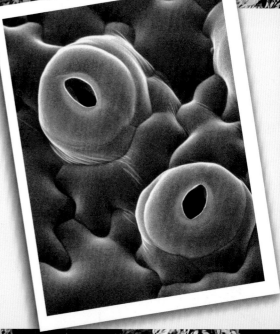

HOT, HOT, HOT!

A tropical rain forest is as hot as a greenhouse, with temperatures normally about 75 °F (24 °C). The nights are almost as warm. Trees do not lose their leaves, so rain forests stay green all year.

MONSOON FORESTS

Some other jungles are monsoon forests. These forests lie in the paths of changeable winds called monsoons, which bring heavy rain storms at certain times. Trees in monsoon forests lose their leaves in the dry season. They grow new leaves when the rains return.

LUSH PLANT LIFE

THE WARM, wet conditions make rain forests the best places in the world to grow plants. You may have noticed how fast plants grow during a warm, rainy summer. Rain forest plants grow as fast as that all year round! One-fifth of the world's plants grow in rain forests.

CROWDED FORESTS

There is a wide variety of trees in rain forests. About 200 different **species** of trees grow in just 2.5 acres (1 hectare) of forest. That compares to about ten different types in a woodland growing in a colder place. Each rain forest tree is home to up to 50 species of smaller plants, and hundreds of different animals, including insects, spiders, birds, frogs, snakes, and monkeys.

▲ *Vines hang down from branches, filling the space below the trees.*

MADE IN LAYERS

Rain forests are divided into layers called stories. Tall trees called emergents form the top layer. Below that, **average**-sized trees spread their branches to form a thick, leafy layer called the canopy. The understory is made up of shrubs on the forest floor.

In the Extreme

The strangler fig sprouts high on a tree from a seed dropped by a bird or monkey. This **parasitic** plant sends roots down to the ground, which steal the **host** tree's moisture. The fig's woody stems wrap around the tree, strangling it to death. The tree trunk rots away leaving a hollow cage of fig stems.

SEA OF GREEN

The main colors in a rain forest are many shades of green. From above, the forest resembles a green, fluffy blanket. Purple and scarlet flowers bloom high in the canopy, but there are few flowers at ground level. Young leaves are sometimes red (*left*), which makes them less attractive to leaf-eating animals.

DRIP TIPS

There are short but heavy rain showers in rain forests nearly every day. The leaves of most trees have a waterproof wax surface and many end in points called drip tips. Drip tips make it easier for water to trickle off the leaf, so trees do not get very wet and moldy.

UPPER LAYERS

The tallest trees in the rain forest are hit by extreme weather. They are blasted by storm winds, drenched by rain, and then scorched in the Sun.

PROTECTION

Conditions are more protective in the canopy below. Here, trees spread their leaves to form a thick green layer above the ground. The leaves collect most of the light and moisture, leaving little for the layers below.

Vital Statistics

★ Emergent trees (*below*) grow to be 230 feet (70 m) tall. Other trees are about 150 feet (45 m) tall.

★ Tualang trees in Southeast Asia are some of the world's tallest trees.

★ Tualang trees have straight trunks and tops shaped like umbrellas.

LIFE AT THE TOP

Until recently, scientists knew
very little about life in the canopy.
Biologists now string walkways
between trees to study the wildlife
in the canopy. Some scientists
winch up and down on climbers'
ropes, while others work from
cranes. Thousands of new species
of plants and animals have been
discovered in the canopy that
are never seen on the ground.

▼ *The canopy in a rain forest is so thick
that you cannot see the ground through it.*

FAST FACTS

★ Plants called epiphytes,
or air plants, do not grow
on the ground. They grow on
branches high in the canopy.

★ Bromeliads are epiphytes
that trap rain in cup-shaped
leaves. Insects and even tiny
frogs breed in these
miniature pools.

In the Extreme

PITCHER PLANTS grow in poor soil in swampy rain forests. The plants get extra **nutrients** from insects. Flies and beetles that land on the edges of the plants slide down the slippery sides into pools of juice. The juice **digests** the insects. The largest pitchers measure one foot (30 cm) long and hold 0.5 gallons (two liters) of liquid.

LOWER LAYERS

The understory of the forest receives far less light and moisture than the layers above. Less than five percent of sunlight shines through the canopy. Raindrops take about ten minutes to filter through the leaves and plop onto the ground. The forest floor is very dark and gloomy. Few large plants grow there, but moss and ferns sprout in clearings or by rivers. A thick carpet of dead leaves covers the ground.

POOR SOIL

Surprisingly, rain forest soil is thin and not very **fertile**, because trees and plants take all the nutrients. Areas beside rivers are more fertile. During the rainy season, rivers burst their banks and spread nutrient-rich mud over the land.

RACE FOR LIGHT

When a huge tree crashes to the ground, it creates a patch of sunlight. Tree seedlings sprout and race upward to spread their leaves and fill the gap in the canopy. As the tree grows taller, its roots fan out at the base of the trunk. These buttress roots work like the supports on old buildings to spread the giant tree's heavy weight.

▼ *The trunk of a large forest tree is surrounded by saplings—young trees that are ready to take its place.*

Vital Statistics

★ The largest flower in the world is *Rafflesia* (*left*) from the forests of Southeast Asia.

★ The flower is more than three feet (one m) wide and weighs 33 pounds (15 kg).

★ The flowers give off a disgusting smell, like rotting meat. This attracts flies that help the plant to reproduce.

RAIN FOREST ANIMALS

RAIN FORESTS contain more types of animals than any other habitat. A huge number of animals have not yet been identified. The reason why rain forests have so many species is that they are very ancient. Over many generations, new species have evolved to survive in the conditions of a particular part of the forest.

▼ Flying frogs from Southeast Asia cannot really fly, but they can glide between trees by spreading their large webbed feet to slow their fall.

LIVING THE HIGH LIFE

Most animals live high in the canopy because that is where most of the fruits, leaves, and other food is. Visiting the canopy is easy for flying creatures, such as birds, bats, and insects. Other animals have to be skilled climbers. Squirrels and monkeys balance with the help of their long tails. Frogs and lizards scale the trees using ridged pads on their toes to grip the bark.

In the Extreme

Sloths eat leaves that have few nutrients. The sloth saves energy by sleeping for 18 hours a day. Its long claws hook over branches, so it does not fall as it goes to sleep. Some sloths are so lazy their fur goes green with mold!

TREE KANGAROOS

Kangaroos are famous for being high-speed hoppers with long back feet. However, the rain forests of New Guinea have kangaroos that live high in trees. Their curving claws help with climbing, but are no use for hopping on the ground. Tree kangaroos are still good at jumping—they can leap 60 feet (18 m) to the ground.

Vital Statistics

✱ Gibbons are small apes that live in Southeast Asian rain forests.

✱ They use their very long arms and slender fingers to swing through the trees at 30 miles per hour (50 km/h)!

✱ Gibbon families spend most of their time in the branches. Each family has its own feeding **territory**, and warns other groups away with shrieks.

✱ Bonobos are small, slender apes with black faces and long limbs. They are also called pygmy chimpanzees.

✱ The rare bonobos live in West Africa. They are thought to be the closest living relatives to humans.

✱ Bonobos are very clever. They live in large groups. They collect fruit and seeds and can even catch fish!

BRAINY BEASTS

Animals that live high in the canopy have to make quick decisions all the time. They have to judge distances with great accuracy as they leap from branch to branch. They also have to keep an eye out for danger, which may come from any direction. The canopy is constantly changing, as leaves sprout and different fruits ripen. Forest animals have to be quick-thinking and have vivid memories to survive.

▲ *Langurs from India are the champion jumpers of the monkey world. They can leap 30 feet (10 m)!*

◄ Chimpanzees are one of the few animals other than humans to use tools.

In the Extreme

The aye aye is a lemur—a type of primate from Madagascar. The weird-looking aye aye hunts grubs living in wood. It uses its long middle finger to hook fat, juicy grubs from the bark.

LAND OF PRIMATES

The world's most intelligent animals—apes and monkeys—live in rain forests. These animals belong to a group of **mammals** called primates along with small species like lemurs. Human beings are also primates! Primates have large, forward-facing eyes, long, muscular limbs, and grasping toes and fingers. Some monkeys have **prehensile** tails that act like fifth limbs. Like people, primates live in groups and take great care of their young.

LIFE IN THE LOWER LAYERS

The lower layers of the forest are less crowded than the canopy. They contain larger animals, however. Many animals have natural disguises, or **camouflage**. Their brown or green colors and spotted, striped, or blotchy markings blend in with the plants and shadows, making them almost invisible. Deadly snakes and huge, hairy spiders may be lurking very close among the leaves!

TAPIRS

Tapirs are pig-like mammals from the Amazon rain forest and parts of Southeast Asia. They love water and use their long, flexible snouts as snorkels. Malaysian tapirs have black and white markings.

▼ The rose-shaped pattern on this jaguar's body helps it stay hidden among the spots of light and shade on the forest floor.

LEAFCUTTER ANTS

Long lines of leafcutter ants march up trunks to harvest leaves from the treetops. They snip leaves with sharp jaws and carry them back to the nest. The ants cut off about ten percent of all forest leaves. The ants do not eat the leaves. They use them to grow a **fungus** garden deep inside the nest. The ants then eat the fungus.

FALLING FOOD

Animals that live on the ground, such as deer and tapirs, eat fruits and seeds that fall from the treetops. Insects, slugs, and worms are recyclers. They feed on the remains of dead plants and animals, helping them rot away.

FAST FACTS

★ Rare rhinos live in the forests of India and Indonesia.

★ Some Asian rhinos have just one horn—African ones have two.

★ Experts think these Asian rhinos **inspired** the legend of the unicorn.

Tarsiers are tiny **nocturnal** primates from Southeast Asia. They look for insects in the dark using their huge eyes. Their sensitive eyes are bigger than their brains.

THE NIGHT SHIFT

Some rain forest animals are active by day. Others hunt for food at night, or during dusk and dawn. Nocturnal animals have enormous eyes to collect enough light to see. Others have strong senses of smell and hearing. Pythons and vipers are snakes with heat-sensitive pits on their faces. The pits allow them to pinpoint warm bodies in the dark.

Vital Statistics

★ The Goliath tarantula is the world's largest spider.

★ The spiders are 11 inches (28 cm) across.

★ The Tarantulas prey on insects, frogs, lizards, birds, and small mammals.

KILLER SNAKE

Vine snakes are in disguise as jungle vines while searching for prey such as lizards, frogs, and mice. They take aim with the help of keyhole-shaped eyes and grooves on the snout that are lined up with the target. The snakes kill with venom that works very quickly so their victims do not struggle free and then fall out of the tree—and out of reach.

CYCLE OF LIFE

All living things are part of the great cycle of life in a rain forest. Plants form the base of **food chains**. They are food for many animals including insects, birds, monkeys, and elephants. Small plant-eaters are food for **carnivores,** such as jaguars, snakes, and eagles. When animals die, their remains are broken down by fungi and bacteria. This returns nutrients to the soil and to forest plants—and so the cycle begins again.

RAIN FORESTS AND PEOPLE

People have lived in rain forests for thousands of years. Many different groups live comfortably in this extreme environment. The forest provides all their needs—food, clothing, medicine, and materials to build homes and tools.

In the Extreme

People in South American jungles use the poison in frog skin to coat darts and arrows used for hunting.

FOOD AND SHELTER

In rain forests across the world, people traditionally live by hunting animals for meat and fishing in local rivers. They also gather plants such as fruits, roots, and nuts. Groups such as the Yanomami of the Amazon and the Huli of New Guinea have gardens in the forest. They grow yams and maize. Traditional homes are huts thatched with leaves. Villages are often along rivers, which provide transportation.

LAB WORK

Rain forest people track animals by looking for their footprints and other clues such as hair and droppings. You can use similar techniques to track animals in a forest. Listen for animal noises and look for tracks in soft mud, such as by a stream, or in the snow.

▶ An Amazon woman has colored her face with paints made from plants.

LITTLE PEOPLE OF THE CONGO

Baka and Mbuti people live in the Congo rain forest in Central Africa. The adults are normally less than five feet (152 cm) tall and they are also known as Pygmies, meaning "small people." The Congo people traditionally hunt with bows.

In the Extreme

In the 16th century, many Amazon peoples fled to remote western areas to escape being attacked by European settlers. They have remained hidden from the rest of the world ever since. Experts think that there are about 50 lost tribes in the forests of Brazil and Peru. They live in ways that have not changed for centuries.

EUROPEANS ARRIVE

Begining in the 15th century, European explorers traveled through the world's rain forests. They were looking for riches such as gold and rare spices. Explorers battled their way through the dense jungles, often following wide rivers upstream. The newcomers found travel difficult. The stifling heat and **humidity** was exhausting. They were attacked by blood-sucking mosquitoes and leeches. Many were even killed by snakes and diseases.

▼ European explorers found cities such as Palenque, built by the Mayans, in Mexico.

TEMPLE CITY

Angkor Wat in Cambodia was built in the 14th century. It is half temple and half city and was once the capital of a thriving empire. Today, tourists come to marvel at the ruins, which are partly overgrown by jungle. The five towers of one temple represent sacred peaks that were home to the Hindu gods.

TROUBLED TIMES

In the centuries that followed, outsiders decided to take over the forest lands. The newcomers harvested **resources**, such as natural rubber, hardwood lumber, gold, and diamonds. Local people were often driven off their lands. Many thousands died from new diseases brought by the Europeans.

▶ *Wealthy tourists came to African forests to hunt large animals.*

In the Extreme

The Ciudad Perdita, meaning Lost City in Spanish, lies in the heart of a dense jungle in Colombia, South America. The ruins perched high above a river were discovered in the 1970s by treasure hunters. Built around 800 A.D., the Lost City includes about 80 stone platforms where huts once stood, linked by paved paths.

MANY CHANGES

In the last 50 years, rain forest plants, animals, and people have come under great threat. Huge areas of rain forest have been cut down. Trees are cut down for lumber and forest is also cleared for farming or mining. Forests are also destroyed as dammed rivers make artificial lakes. In addition, new communities brought new ways of life with them. People now realize that the forests should be protected. Local groups have been given control of their lands and national parks protect forest wildlife.

▼ *Every year, an area the size of Florida is cut down in the world's rain forests.*

In the Extreme

Rain forests are dangerous. Most people who get lost there never make it home. However, there are some amazing tales of survival. In 1971, German teenager Juliane Koepcke was stranded in the Amazon when her plane crashed. She remembered her father's advice: head downhill to find a river, which should lead to civilization. After ten days in the forest, Juliane stumbled into a hunter's camp and was rescued.

LAB WORK

Rain forests provide a huge number of products we use in everyday life. Foods such as bananas, pineapples, sugar, coffee, and chocolate (from cacao pods, *right*) all start out in rain forests or in places that were once covered in forest. Hardwoods, such as teak, used to make furniture also come from forests. How many rain forest products can you find at home?

MAKING CONTACT

Scientists estimate that around 1,000 different groups of people live in rain forests around the world. These include about 100 cultures that have not had contact with outsiders for hundreds of years. Care is taken when outside people first visit these remote villages. They must avoid giving the forest tribe diseases or disturbing their ways of life.

COUNTDOWN

Although the rain forest is full of life, outsiders can get into trouble and starve. If you are not prepared, you will soon get wet, tired, and hungry. Pack a first-aid kit, a machete for cutting vines, maps, compass, food, water-purifying tablets, and a hammock. Wear boots and long trousers to protect against leeches and snake bites, and take spare clothes in a waterproof bag.

EXTREME FACTS

PLANT POISON

Amazon people use a plant poison called curare to coat their darts and arrows. Curare is used in **anesthetics** to relax patients' muscles before operations.

LARGEST LEAF

The Amazon water lily (*right*) produces the world's largest leaves, up to six feet (two m) across. The lily leaves float on water and are strong enough to support the weight of a person.

EXPLORER'S ACCOUNT

Christopher Columbus provided the first written account of a rain forest, from the Caribbean island of Hispaniola. He wrote, "The land is filled with trees of a thousand kinds and so tall, they seem to touch the sky."

A TIGHT SQUEEZE

The anaconda, the world's largest snake, lurks in the muddy rivers of South America. It is big enough to kill and eat a caiman—a type of alligator.

RAIN FOREST CITY

Manaus is the largest town in the South American rain forest. It lies at a junction where two huge rivers join to make the Amazon. Ocean-going ships can travel 1,000 miles upriver to this busy port.

KILLER BIRD

The world's most dangerous bird is the cassowary of New Guinea. The five-foot (1.5 m) bird runs through the forest. It has a pointed bone, or casque, on its head, which helps it slice through the undergrowth. The casque also protects the bird when it hits a tree trunk—or person. Cassowaries have been known to slash people with five-inch (12 cm) claws.

MAN–APE

The orangutan (*above*) is a large forest ape from Borneo and Sumatra. It is covered with long red fur. The name *orangutan* means "Man of the Forest."

LOST IN THE JUNGLE

In 2007, two Frenchmen planned an 11-day hike through untouched forest in the Amazon. But they became lost and eventually ran out of food. Hungry and exhausted, they made camp and survived by eating bugs and poisonous spiders. Finally one of the men made a last, desperate attempt to reach help, only to find they had camped just 2.5 miles (four km) from a town!

FAST GROWER

Bamboo (*above*) is the world's fastest-growing plant. The giant bamboo can grow over three feet (one m) in one day.

GLOSSARY

anesthetics Drugs used to make people sleep or feel no pain during surgery

average A normal amount that is not too small and not too large

carnivores Animals that eat meat

digest To break up food into smaller, more useful substances

equator The imaginary line that runs around the middle of Earth

evaporate When water (or another liquid) turns into a gas, such as steam

fertile Able to support life or produce young

food chains Patterns of eating and being eaten

fungus A type of living thing that includes mushrooms and molds

host A plant or animal that has another plant or animal living on or inside of it

humidity A measure of how much water vapor there is in the air

inspired Given an idea for something

mammals A group of animals that have hairy bodies and feed young with milk

moisture Small amounts of water in the environment

nocturnal Active at night

nutrients Vitamins, minerals, and other things needed for growth

parasitic To live as a parasite—surviving by stealing food and drink from another plant or animal

prehensile Able to grab things

resources Materials that are useful to humans, such as metal, wood, and oil

species A group of animals that are very closely related to each other. Members of one species can breed; living things from two different species cannot

territory An area animals consider theirs

tropical From the tropics—warm and wet regions of the world

water vapor Steam; water as a gas

winch Lifting and lowering things on a strong rope

FURTHER RESOURCES

BOOKS

Fading Forests: The Destruction of Our Rainforests by August Greeley. New York, NY: PowerKids Press, 2003.

Hiding in a Rain Forest by Patricia Whitehouse. Chicago, IL: Heinemann Library, 2003.

Life In a Rain Forest by Carol K. Lindeen. Mankato, MN: Capstone Press, 2004.

Rain Forest Animals by Nancy Leber. Minneapolis, MN: Compass Point Books, 2004.

Rainforest Creatures by Benita Sen. New York, NY: PowerKids Press, 2008.

WEBSITES

Jungle Interactive (Draw your own rain forest)

www.nga.gov/kids/zone/jungle.htm

National Geographic Rain Forest Videos.

video.nationalgeographic.com/video/player/environment/
habitats-environment/rainforests

Rain forest Hereos (Rain forest Action Network)

ran.org/rainforestheroes

INDEX

Printed in the U.S.A. — BG